Dedication:
To my mother

Saffron Rosa
by
John Dedham

Saffron
Rosa

1. Jinxed

Tonight, the stars are bright, look through the eye of a telescope
explore the colossal mystery of the Universe;
adjust the focal length, align the plates
listen to the jive of the Milky Way.

Sight zooms along dusty lanes across space and time
to the star-lit centre of the galaxy;
see hot suns nascent in birth, nebulous
clouds of pregnant gas sculpted
over aeons by solar-winds as particles ionise,
gravitate into dense matter of base metals
the lead weight of giant planets suspended in space;
see the frozen flash of super-novas
the soft ripple of spectacular explosions
as suns collide, collapse into white-dwarfs
radiation, thermal heat, echoes of empty chambers
the dust inchoate with dense starry clusters.

Waves of ultra-sound can penetrate this brightness
zoom-in to the heart of the Milky Way
this spiralling spangled wheel of light;
calibrate the sensors, compute the data
heaven help us! what strange palpitations
oscillate at its very centre!
an impenetrable dense mass of magnetic anti-matter
as space and time collapse
into a black vortex of annihilation
that devours everything, nothing can escape
a vacuum at the very centre of creation!

All suffering is the suffering of God;
the human heart that beats
the human heart that bleats
its terrestrial distress

between being and nothingness,
a new birth opens another door
as dawn radiates her celestial colours
and white mists cloak sweet water-meadows
a golden sun wrestles this devil to the floor
of tangible, intangible godlessness.

2. The Universal You

'You're all alone in the universe
a reality that makes no sense
galaxies of bright hypnotic stars
teem with indifference.

You're all alone in a daily farce
what is real and what pretence?
reveals as the script unfolds
that Life bludgeons innocence.

You're all alone in a crowded tube
with people that you do not know
walking quick through indifferent streets
to the isolation of your home.

You're all alone with the ones you love
they do not know who you are at all!
but most of all when you're by yourself
with the stranger that you call your soul.'

3. Mind

Nature has a mind, it is not our own;
from amino-acids to single cells
evolving into compounds and molecules
mutating with infinite variations
into teeming biological organisms
each programmed by a gentic bind
to inviolable laws of evolution
whole species destroyed in mass extinction
nature has a mind; it is not our own.

Automata have a mind, it is not our own;
a utopia for science seeking salvation
through technological evolution
artificial intelligence devoid of emotion
operating with micro-chip precision
in an existential vacuum
programmed to weapons of mass destruction
could incinerate an entire civilisation
automota have a mind; it is not our own.

God has a mind, it is not our own;
suspended in the vacuum of space and time
without any apparent plan or design
an invisible face in the inky heavens
incommensurable, ex-machina
as cosmic particles in random scatter
an oscillating waves riding dark matter
a dance of chaos, as mad as a hatter
god has a mind; it is not our own

People have a mind, it is not their own;
housed in a casement of fragile bone
biological, a globular hemisphere

of chemical synapsis and dark primal fear
prone to injury, memory, decay,
the font of all personality
that disappears into the white mist
of human subjective consciousness
people have a mind; it is not their own

4. A Workman's Complaint

From out of a large housing estate complex
a worker approaches, angry and shouting
his voice reproaching with brutal rant
the empty walkways of the evening-

'I'm a hooman bein'.....'

Clad in jeans, donkey-jacket and boots
with a large lumpy forehead and small frightened eyes
he hates his job, his home, his wife
but most of all he hates his life-

'I'm a hooman bein'..... so shut it!
you don't know nuffin' about it.....'

He stops, now speechless
insignificant by an urban freeway
lost in the geometry of the evening,
an earthworm muscles beneath the asphalt;
obliquely, a lurid sunset casts
darkness behind each squat building.

His only deity is television
that knows his dreams, his earthly desires
the secret turmoil of his soul –
'Jesus Wept!....' he begins
disoriented and vehement,
'its an endless maze in which we live.....'

5. The Working Class

You dispossessed and working classes
confined to warehouse and to factory
you are the foundation of Society
who pick the harvests, build the houses
produce the goods that run the State.

For a weekly wage that lasts one week
so week by week your life erodes
a life you cannot choose or own
but clock-off and clock-on
as your daily shift dictates.

Oppressed by tedium and hard labour
subservient to the sterile machine
without tenure or security
your soul atrophies from salvation
your only redemption, Revolution.

6. A Change of Address

'Destiny – destinations
a change of address
driving through the suburbs
memory boiling away
like water in a pan –

Driving through the suburbs
into mystical dawn
a slow birth of light…..
but the Golden Automobile
once ignited, must needs record Time…..

What exigencies – what expediences?
driven through life
to a sun-struck sidewalk
of place and time
as cars slew past.

Turning into an avenue
a change of address
leading to further avenues –
Utopias
sweet absolutes of happiness!....

Exteriors – interiors
the memory smoulders
a sun struck street –
mad files trapped behind net curtains
in closed rooms.

A baby's cry, a block of flats
in a parking-lot
a car-siren detonates
heartbeat
pulsating in the heat.

Turning into another avenue
home is –
which direction?
opportunities missed or falsely won
parallel routes forsaken.

The map misread, the turning lost
no recognition
on an estate of identical facades
the roads confused, the signs mute
to the Avenue of Absolutes.

Turning into an avenue
the final address
blank reminiscence –
streets, doors, numbers, windows
pavements, kerbs, bricks, glass –

Transfixed in a cul-de-sac
of sun-struck tarmac
no identity
memory boiling away
like water in a pan –'

7. Amnesia

'One part of a fragment –
                              a foetal position
consciousness; daylight
                              trapped in a living room
an eye unemotional
                              as radar, registers
white mist of net-curtain
leaf-pattern of wallpaper
                              the sofa a womb
staring down the stare of insane creation
that is just 'there'
the mind waits and watches
                              silent and still
like any animal trapped in a snare;
hours drift by
                              as formless as clouds
flat walls of daylight are just as unreal.

One part of a fragment –
                              a foetal position
consciousness; the penumbra
                              of evening
crosses the ceiling
                              gathers in corners
as night creeping forward
lights the one glowing
                              eye of nirvana
housed in a circuit of micro-chip cells;
a paradise of colour
                              without taste or smell
realities that move in their own dimension
animate a heaven
                              without pain or desire
the paralysed soul's lost requiem.'

8. Suburbs

An early morning heat haze
vibrant over pavement and suburb rose
bored houses, idling daylight
dazed by sodium street lighting
its yellow sickness lit the dawn.

Streets stunned with heat
in a swelter of silence;
metallic cars glitter
parked on scorched tarmac
behind sheets of frosted glass

Rooms close with a stifling heat
an ice-cream van cruising the estate
booms a chiming mechanical refrain
inanely into the soulless heat;
the eyes are the source of a dark river…..

9. The Estate

A finite world has finite resources;
new factories were planned to serve the estates
built on the periphery of cities, to provide
every family with a job and a home
demographic curve of future populations
disconnected from nature's organic laws
of cycle and growth; no season of harvest
on the estates when local factories close,
precipitated by the collapse of financial markets,
then unemployment precedes social malaise –
daytime T.V., drugs and alcohol abuse
the placebo of the computer and the video
(when Virtual Reality becomes too real)
the escape of wheels and the smell of petrol;
no career, except a car careering
around the estate, pursued by the police
into a crowded street of parked cars;
a bang of metal and shattering of glass
shuddering to a stop 2 youths run off
abandoning a young girl inside who weeps…..

10. Sons

Boy Racers tear around the estates in stolen cars,
their wheel-skids burn in the night
under cover of darkness, taunting the police
in a ritual of male bonding with shaved heads,
gold-earrings, tattoos, warrior chic
chased around urban conurbations
that once were rural retreats,
old farmsteads, rough cottages, now sealed
under tarmac, a matrix of roads
as complex as the history that spawned
their lives, racing the circuits
with reckless speed, a testosterone high,
then a dent, a smash, a deliberate crash
and to prove a full-on ego, the car
set ablaze, a burning conflagration
to proclaim the ardour of their disaffection.....

11. Daughter

When the car mounted the pavement
just after school hours, on an average
suburban street, one parent and two children
were knocked aside, with bruised limbs
and some breakage (Boy Racer has misjudged
the corner) but a third child,
a little girl walking home, was directly in the path.
The car mounted the kerb, then
mounted her, as it skid to a halt.
Underneath the chrome she lay prostrate
(with a split upper-lip), clutching
her satchel in her hand,
and died of internal injuries
just as the ambulance arrived.
Bouquets of withering flowers now mark
the site, tied to the railings
suffering the passage of time
the sun and the showers
and the passing feet of strangers…..

12. Mother

'My little girl's heart no longer beats our drum
of love; the sun rising through our house
will not wake her from her bed, my little dove
her sleepy head upon my shoulder as we walk
the quite carpets from room to room.
Tender curled fingers, soft hair
eye-lids closed around a dream
her name a sound unspoken now
the empty hollow of our home
waiting for her name to sound.
Her vacant room is tidy, neat
with toys unplayed; this day that is bereft
of her and all the future years
bereft of her laughter and her tears
never to see her growing up, never
to welcome her home from school, never
to take her to the shops, help her
try my make-up on….. my little girl,
our love was severed in an instant…..
my heart is grief; grief is my heart
my grief could darken the sun of the world;
all the deceased songbirds of time
warbling in a dark cellar
mourn the loss of my little girl…..'

13. Father

'I, as automatic as a machine
shut in the unit of a factory
sealed-in by vertical sterile walls
clocking-off and clocking-on
synchronised to a machine
incessant rapture of noise and din
in a perpetual neon-lit present
where real time has ceased to exist
morning, noon, evening or night
with only the next, next, next
infernal repetition of work…..
it was my little girl you slaughtered
my resolve is hard and strong
now my shift is nearly over
I will find out where you live
Boy Racer, you will not live long…..'

14. Youth

'Youth, youth, fly with me
I'm Master of the Ceremony
be anything you want to be
youth, youth, fly with me.….

Dance, dance in ecstasy
be king of all reality
wing through eternity
dance, dance in ecstasy.….

Youth, youth fly with me
yours is a golden destiny
be anything you want to be,
youth, youth, fly with me.….

Dance, dance in ecstasy
I'm Master of the Ceremony
wing through eternity
dance, dance in ecstasy.…'

15. Shadows

With your elongated arms and legs, unusually thin
like some strange stick-insect seen in an aquarium
unemployed and unemployable
you stalk the streets, clad in denim
looking for a daily routine
to give some meaning to your existence
partitioned behind a pane of invisible glass.

Your eyes are apprehensive, set behind a face
vulnerable, accustomed to intimidation
from life's giant arbitrary shadows
in your past and in the present;
a humiliating childhood, your parent's divorce
'I never asked to come here', you had said,
you disown them now.

With no social roots, only a series
of bedsit rooms and temporary accommodation
where you have had to roost, like a
stricken animal in a secreted lair,
life is no struggle towards salvation
but mere survival, the next social security cheque
or the home you search for, that you never had.

16. The Protagonist

Rapper is animal, Rapper is jest
he's poor and dangerous, without an address
roams restless thoroughfares, dark city streets
rapscallion skeleton, blood on heat
his skull ethereal with eternal desire
for life and lust and a sun on fire
a red heart that is empty of god;
as evening crowds jostle in twilight mutations
teeming and parting to pre-destinations
engulfed in the throng of giant-lit stores
displayed in glass windows of heavenly visions
all the wealth and luxury society can proffer
Rapper scorches with the mental fires
of his mind's methane imaginary flames
evangelic….. barbaric….. arithmetic…..
coursing through the curse of his life
as lives criss-cross in the proselytising dark
in a night's incoherence, the constant question –

'dancing horses, dancing horses
they dance around, prance on frozen ground……'

In the deeps of night burn alphabets of neon
lacquering the structure of geometric buildings
angled and tangled, lambent, incumbent
lost in a multi-storied blackness
Rapper starving smells
the benison of the venison, rich savoury gravy
flavouring his cravings; hungering down streets
passed by the arc of glowering cars
unhoused, elemental, eyeing the basements

'who has a key to open all doors
when all doors open into closed rooms?
one room contains the happiness of human lives
one room is furnished with desolation
one room is a silent swirling cosmos
but who has a key to open all doors
the golden key to a golden existence?'

'dancing horse, dancing horses
they dance around, prance on frozen ground…..'

High in the depth of frozen night
the super-structure of a crane towers
its long jaw scatters fleeting shadows
articulating beneath the rings of a brittle moon
its pendulum slowly swivels, icy bright –
the absence and presence of the living
the absence and presence of the dead.

'dancing horses, dancing horses
they dance around, prance on frozen ground…..'

Above the metropolis, in silent abstraction
snow-flakes take shape, silently fall
into the night, out of the night;
a snow-flake alights upon Rapscallion's skull
'Be still, and know that I am God'
as snow-flakes in thick multitudes descend
settle onto the silence of fresh fallen snow
Rapper sleeps deep beneath a blanket of white
disappears into a blizzard of dazzling light.

'dancing horses, dancing horses
they dance around, prance on broken ground
dancing horses, dancing horses
they dance on cars, kick the frozen stars
they shatter frozen time to smithereens!'

17. Urban Chiaroscuro

In draughty sheds on isolated farms
cattle rest their bulk in deep litters of straw
chew fodder with vacant eyes, some cough
frosting their breath on the frozen air;
soon they'll be dismembered into joints of meat
displayed upon counters in bright-lit stores
where hungry crowds surge in the evening
beneath neon lights in glass office-towers.

Televisions flicker in bold front windows
on suburb estates, illuminate reality
in a blur of images as families sit
transfixed in their halos, cars zoom
over concrete flyovers, past dense populations
hidden behind uniform facades;
in a glittering shop-window of an empty arcade
in fluorescent nirvana, television talk.

In the chiaroscuro of an urban district
violence, tenantless, roams in the street
enter the flats and rides in the lift
fists clenched around a dull blunt knife;
on the scroll of a motorway, carrion unfolds
blood-lights of an artery of cars
pulling over by a pavement verge
a malcontent approaches with slow burning eyes
'Quick! Drive on!.....'

18. A Holy Fool

A 'dark god' or a holy fool?
strides purposefully down the centre
of the corso, through sheets of driving rain
the storm clouds swirling
behind his head, engulfing the mountains
dramatically darkening packed city-streets;
his eyes transfixed, oblivious
to speeding automobiles that pass
close on either side, his figure
upright, tall and statuesque
like a fearless colossus he strides
forwards into the traffic and pelting rain.

Dreadlocks platted into a crown
with sacks tied around both feet and ankles
he splashes through the puddles
washed-out from the stink of neighbouring ghettos
soiled, muffled in rags, not limping;
nights spent on cardboard and hard stone-cobbles
numbed weary limbs
the pangs of hunger, the rats scurrying.

His eyes are defiant
his mind like a cavernous opera-house
filled with crescendos of arias
he looks straight ahead
towards a heaven only he can see
in his pride, his glory, his agony.

19. Populations

'Populations bubble, arise and bloom
give me a space, a rented room
measured in cubits of rented air

somewhere where I can stretch a bed
give me four walls, a safe place
unfettered by profit, a fair rent

safe from the furies of avarice and greed
the slavering mongrel capitalism feeds;
give me a space, a fair room

somewhere where I can live and breathe
give me the space of the land that I crave
where birds and trees sing free in the breeze.

Population bubble, divide and swarm
give me a space, a rented room
a just rent secure and warm

somewhere where I can stretch a bed
give me four walls, a safe place
the only mortgage that I can afford

will house me in a casket of wood
all my life I am going to save
for a space that is mine; it will be my grave.'

20. Urban Dramas

The alarms start ringing, and the district falls quite
they continue to ring, in an expectant silence
a bridge swings open, at the press of a button.

A muzzled alsatian pads on the pavement
the flats, the spires, stand tall to attention
crowds are milling for a quick bargain.

Shopping, walking, bawling children
the shimmering coiffure of a black Madonna
trays of cakes and trays of bread.

Buddleias sprout purple tongues
where the dead are buried by the river
the hollow eyes of decayed housing.

The great ideal, in collision with concrete and steel
corrugated mud of empty harbours
streets of dark kidney light.

A flood of people, a river of faces
rust of successive generations
in a weird histrionic drama.

Splinters of colour explode in the night
people stop talking, a bridge swings shut
a white fall of snow obliterates it all.

21. Capitalism

'Capitalism is a whore;
she deposits shit of pure gold
banked in dark subterranean vaults

Used on the streets, used and abused
by shirts and ties and suits
who walk the glamorous plazas

Broking deals and smoothing power
high in executive office suites
woo their sweetheart, ravish her

Above the crowded populations
feast on the gravy of their labour
gold bonds, gilt-edged securities

The sweet green sward of nature
gouged open for fiscal profit
of real estate and property

Her rich harvests and her treasure
oppressed by the dull weight of concrete
used on the streets, used and abused

Fed by the greed of a godless culture
she profits the rich, impoverishes the poor
it is Capitalism that is the whore.'

22. The Corridors of Power

They have no love for the common folk
who bred and toiled in fields
sustained by the rhythm of the seasons
un-coupled from the plough and the yoke

By enclosure, then the wilful demise of industry,
their skills and their trades made obsolete
by micro-chip and machine automata;
no harvests on the estates

When local factories close,
production and manufacture
their bread and their butter;
without security and without property

No job, no hope, no power
except what lies within their scope
to defy the elite with insurrection –
how righteous the politician's paranoia…..

23. Blood

It's the ruby stuff, that flows from the crown
from the heels, from the hands
from anywhere it can…..

A cocktail of chemistry
carries personal identity
blueprint of memory.

The diesel that runs the machine
the precious coda for race and genes
catalyst of human history.

Purified by the heart, sealed
in the veins, the liquor
and elixir of life it contains.

Liberated from flesh
flows down the drains
in bomb-ripped streets

Outside schools, by a bus-stop
on the way to a corner-shop
when knives strike in inner-cities

Acts of violence, retribution
programmed by savage
biological evolution.

Once redeemed by the true sweet blood
that ran down a Cross of Wood
of forgiveness and the forgiven.

It's the ruby stuff
that carries all dreams
more precious than gold that lies in seams

It breaks from the crown
from the heels, from the hands
from anywhere it can…..

24. The Human Claw

When first violent impulses of brute nature
recoil from the will's instinctive
survival of the self, teeth full bared
against the vicissitudes of natural selection
not to be victim or prey to a predator;
cornered on the upper deck of a bus
when vulnerable or weakened members
of society, defenceless, vicariously attacked,
wounded and dying, falling, falling to the floor
that's when the hand becomes a claw.

The pulled knife; an inopportune stare;
brute ignorance exempt from individual conscience
of free will aligned to original sin,
then civil liberties breed uncivil blood
issuing from the ghetto of the human mind,
insolence and hatred, human and bleeding
nature's natural violence uncivilised;
when society fails to instruct its progeny
in both divine and human law,
that's when the hand becomes a claw.

25. Burnt Child

Nature is all around us, within us and without us
each person an individual nation-state
whose sovereign consciousness rules the body-politic;
breached by virus, assailed by microbes
when riot and confusion overthrow civil-order
the constitution racked by tribal violence –
now prostrate on a mattress in a basement in an alien land
as benzodiazepines mingle with his blood
his memory cries out –

The smell of smoke from the burning villages
a savage land burnt by a savage sun
fear – in the ruins and shadows of childhood
gunshots split a heartbeat; the glitter of blood
spilt in searing heat, a child's eyes witness
death – flies through the dusk like a giant insect
settles in the dust; an indescribable stench floats-in
from the surrounding scrubland, where corpses lie
hidden and bloated, as death wriggles and writhes beneath the skin.

He stares out at a blank ceiling that is colourless and too low
shipwrecked in a room of claustrophobic heat
tenant without tenure
his eyes are wet, his pupils ticking clocks
the language of his heart is mute with dried blood, mud and rags
surrounded by a wilderness
heat bursts from his brain –
he howls, he ululates, an animal's howl
he howls for his ancestors, his parents, his god
he howls incessantly throughout the long night
a night of endless isolation, waiting
for first light to delineate his curtains,
give shape to the furniture crouched in his room.

Exhausted, he drifts into a lucid dreaming
of gliding water and summer's heaven;
dissolves into a pure ethereal blue
filled with the slender wings of swallows
that swoop and dive
carve out of solar light divine abstractions
crossing and criss-crossing in ellipses of flight
he begins to wake up; Wake Up!
Life is pointing both barrels at you!
outside his window a sweet bird of morning
softly sings her quotidian song…..
'S'cuse me, good morning, is it your birthday?
Good heavens above! Good heavens above!
no love for your sorrow, no love for your sorrow
no love for your sorrow, no love for your sorrow
Good heavens above! Good heavens above!…..'

26. Blind Pegasus

'Hush, approach quietly, do not make a sound
he stands over there, breathing in the dark
behind the bars of his concrete stall
Blind Pegasus, like a statue, stands absolutely still.

Is he listening? his coat is pure white
giant wings, like a swan's, fold across his back
his warm, silent breathing moistens the air
his eyes, liquid jewels, have forsaken their sight.

Is he thinking? immobile with apprehension
his consciousness bound to material realms
the slightest touch of his coat would repel
a swift and sudden violent reaction.

As he stands in darkness and isolation
waiting for light to delineate the real,
waiting to see without sight, will his soul
on transcendental wings take flight?

Flying through cloud over broken mountains
gliding through mist around peaks of granite
reflected in meres of watery mirrors
invisible in vapours of dazzling light.

Hush, approach quietly, do not make a sound
he stands over there, breathing in the dark
behind the bars of his concrete cell
Blind Pegasus, like a stone, stands absolutely still.'

27. Glass Museum

'Time wingeth, mad martyrs!
millions and millions of aeons of time
have fossilised our hearts into dumb stone
our viscera into pouches of heavy crud

Our eyeballs twinned to stone
staring out of a glass museum
our blue skies crushed into layers of shale
in the flicker of an eye-lash

Millions of years wing-by; what to do?
and still mother nature suckles her young
her bounteous bosom
blousy with fauna and flora

Outside the glass cabinet of our exhibition
of pedestrian-life, car-life,
the fat planets
revolve in their different spheres.

Here with the shells, the amphibians
the multitudinous unlucky ones
that once were living,
backbones ossified, mollified

Tissue and softness traced into stone
let's keep present suffering in abeyance
for once in a while nature flares
with mineral beauty; pretend to be sane

Step aside and allow the traffic to pass
there's a bit of luck! through the slush
and whirling snow a juggernaut of light
it's our bus with the magic number on it!'

28. The City

A fresh breeze blows from the river
      carrying ozone to blackened wharves
warehouses expel the breath of sick perfumes.
      A solitary bell vibrates in a courtyard
a burnt-out basement is full of fern.
      Tiers of cavernous scaffold straddle broken streets
plinth to tall siphons of tinted glass
      that lean against a monumental sky.
The silver flash from an electric train
      silhouettes a powerhouse, broad and immense
its drums of machinery smoothly revolving.
      An old man, destitute, with faltering steps
slumps under a railway bridge, against a brick wall.
      A bare tree laden with a choir of shrill starlings
descant insanely in the failing twilight.

Many anxious dawns hang upon the creases
      of his forehead. By day he watches the brisk
activity of human commerce; by night
      bright buses of human desire that drone by,
but to other destinations. He himself is nowhere,
      his soul having subsided. For shelter
he inhabits a great woollen overcoat
      and sips weakened spirits from a bottle.
He converses with the traffic, and this news
      bellows at passing pedestrians –
'You! everyday I read the 'papers…..'
      he staggers, looks around, gesturing
'it's all money!…..' he spreads his hands with sincerity,
      'everything is outta control!…..'

29. War

'Sir! get up! has He overslept?
the world's gone insane! violence and fear
ripple through the realms like a malignant wind
His anguished people lament in vain.

Jesus Wept! is He still in bed? guns are pounding
a city to dust, wake Him up!
or a nuclear bang will be His alarm
but the world will be dead.

No! it's impossible! what's that you say?
there's no one there
only an empty room
filled with a vacancy?

Oh well! never mind!
He'll come back one day
all life is mortal and must end therein,
we'll all be able to have a long lie-in!'

30. Sun

'I waxed my car, my car waxing
with a warm summer's sun
it is red, the engine running
many aeons are left to burn.

On the clock lies the future
on the pedal present fun
in the distance roads converging
close on the focal point of zen.

Speeding over hardened surface
whether straight or meandering
fleeing from time, my petrol emotion
carbonates a hot engine.

I waxed my car, my car waxing
in the glare of a nuclear sun
it is red, my car igniting;
all roads to zero run.'

31. A Father's Lament

'My daughter, when I stop your precious breath
it is because I cannot guide
that cruel vehicle of pitiless chance
that courses upon a road hard metalled with suffering;
unredeemed by faith, annihilated by time
it cruises towards your innocent and tender heart.'

His mind compressed, burnt with despair
as her father climbs the stile he hears
the mill-wheel of nothingness beat in the air
across an open common by a bicycle path
where willows cascade in a river of leaves
his daughter waits with faithful eyes.

32. Nature

Nature you're obscene! from your glutinous womb
spring forth all manner of vile progeny
on sexual heat for your one scheme
to procreate! to procreate!

But an earthworm twists, burning
under an electric sun, raw
with pain. why give birth
into naked day, this worm?

When bursting stars fill the heavens with heat
for life is hooked onto a single thread
crustaceans march in a straight procession
two rows of legs in step, in step…..

When some blind force has bruised
the cellular matter that packs hot skulls
cruelty marches forward
to escape the oppressive heat.

33. A Prophet

'For I am a Prophet, my enlightenment
lights-up the heavens, makes visible the majesty
of all things; the very trees whisper my name
with their keen tongues, for I have sown kingdoms

Like prairies of grass, from a whim I can make
into desert again, for I command the rain;
I can cashier the destruction of vast cities
their denizens scrabbling over heaps of rubble

Its very dust I can commandeer; if I should choose
aeroplanes would plummet to earth from the sky
for I am a prophet, Master of Hell; I rave and I rave
at the sterile walls of this white cell.'

34. The Sword of Truth

'Let the Angel who wields the Sword of Truth
the Archangel who wields the burning sword
flash that sword through the Sin of the World
engulf the world in self-righteous Wrath.

the fires of hell will lick the balls of your feet
the fires of hell will split your doughty heart
the fires of hell will wither your intestines
the fires of hell will crack and blacken your bones

But at least you'll be toasty! For it's quite warm
down there, with no icy blasts to freeze your toes
or Siberian wastes to numb bone-marrow
no stampeding glaciers to gift you the sorrow
of frigid non-existence, of no tomorrow;
with eternal heating at no extra charge
it'll be cozy! a snow-flake in hell?
with an infinity of time for you to rehearse
repentance, salvation, it could be worse!'

35. Baby in Flames

'I bet it hurt
when Baby bounced out of the blue
on a Jumbo-Jet,
when the crashing plane
bounced-off the ground
then burst into flames;
but what use to complain
that Life is Insane
when Baby burst into flames?

I bet it hurt
when a hedgehog cornered by a rat
had each spine gnawed down
to its flesh-root, the meat
devoured with chiselled teeth
bleating with hysteria;
but what use to complain
Carnage of Nature
that Life is Insane?

I bet it hurt
for soldiers fighting in battalions
the slaughter, rape and torture
of people perishing in their millions
in evolution to the future;
but what use to complain
of vicarious pain
to a powerhouse Void
that Life is Insane?'

36. The Joker

The comic cracks another joke
about the latest breaking disaster
the audience collapse in helpless laughter
of divine mirth or near hysterics.

Knowing the absolute finality of death
is too obscene, only an obscene jest
can redeem, with irony, mass sudden death
its apparent arbitrary meaninglessness.

He works the bar with mike in hand
another gag; the audience explode
into bright tears of mirth, unable
to divine any sacred worth

In their irreverent secular existence;
the tragic frailties of human fate
his profane jests can only mock;
outside the bar, Creation waits.

37. Natural Laws

Beyond the tree-line, beyond the Sun
big violence is going on
through the infinite tides of space
planets crash, in blindness, break.

It's nothing personal; only a clause
of nature's inexorable laws
so ticks the inter-stellar clock
of floating ice and stones and rock.

38. Loose Horse

Loose horse! loose horse! the idiot cries
through none can understand his words
a frantic mime of hands and sounds
cannot explain his earnest fears.

Loose horse! loose horse! It's now too late
to contain beast with fence and post
a dark physique has trotted past
lurches through an open gate.

Loose horse! the mindless terror
of a drifting universe
dislocate in time and space
irrevocable acts of sordid error.

Muscle, sheath and tendon
driven by a material will
on the open road of its own law
without a moral codicil.

Loose horse! a corn-haired whore
drops her sin into the world
one day her child will kill in hate
fixed upon its wheel of fate.

As teaming nature multiplies
generates increase of grief
puzzle-pieces will not lock
into a vision of belief.

Panic on the verge of midnight
brute genetic laws are blind
a riderless horse gallops on
disconnected from the mind.

Loose horse! loose horse! the idiot's strife
runs too late to shut the gate
death will not reconcile
the vicissitudes of his life.

Loose horse! loose horse! nature's sweets
one day will perish intestate
when the stars shine, the signals flash
the sun pops and the Earth cremates.

39. Garden of Eden

By the sides of a dense and muscular river
a cold and swollen body of water
sweeps past the edge of the barren marshes
their banks oily with effluence and ooze.

Beached on the shore by a receding high tide
lie skiens of trash and human detritus
like the sinuous body of a many coloured snake
washed-up from the world's tidal flood

Bright with the ornament of coloured plastics
emptied of their toxic waste
a serpent from a lost Garden of Eden
sickens this land with its slow poison.

40. Rain

Rain in early evening falls
rivers swell to full flood;
light drowns under lowering cloud
coiling along forlorn mountains
that loom over forests of sullen pine,
their fissured faces split with age.

A white torrent pours
frozen on a mountain-side
robust winds ruffle
banks of buoyant fern;
on a black lake
scudding white-waves race to the shore.

41. Nowhere

'There was no grave
that rainy day
nothing to be found
no scudding clouds
no shuddering skies
nothing in the ground.

There were no bones
that rainy day
no people to be found
no human face
no human race
buried in the ground.

There were no birds
that rainy day
air without a sound
no whispered words
no spoken vowels
frozen in the ground.

There was no grace
that rainy day
no heaven to be found
no redeeming love
within, without
nothing all around.'

42. Lady Death

She was sitting bolt upright in bed
in her room at the top of the stairs
beaming with a benign smile
the door of her room left wide open
the policy of the care-home.

It was the shock of her death's-head
that greeted visitors ascending the stairs
her almost hairless crown
with skin like parchment, a living skull
grinning with an unearthly stare.

Her frail, desiccated, wizened torso
revealed ribs, limbs and bones
more skeletal than human
wrapped in a flimsy cotton-gown
kept alive by medication

And the nurses dedicated care
at the close of a very long life
with loss of memory, cognizance, sense,
and a strange diminishing humanity –
to the final impersonality of Death.

43. Yesterdays

'We hear their voices, see their faces
as the mind's inner reflection traces
their memories that lick like flames
through the living greenwood of our brains.

Woodsmoke of reminiscences
engender into life their forms again
particular idiosyncrasies
of movement, speech and gesture.

Their being that is non-existent
their presence we cannot embrace
familiars as invisible as air
they are not there! they are not there!'

44. Fool's Chant

'My love is ash
like the sun above
for just one day
bring back my love.

An electric storm
flares in my head
a hanging man
swings from a shed.

My love is ash
she has no face
a gob of fire
burns in space.

A victim is screaming
a scare in the dark
unsure of its meaning
the guard dogs bark.

My love is ash
consumed by a flame
like the burning One
that has no name.

Let the restless ocean
cease its strife
let the Earth in motion
find paradise.'

45. Earth Loom

Where is Wendy? the wind flaps
Wendy, Wendy
where is she?
the sun warm on her brown neck.

Steaming cooking pots, torn sack
here is the floor
on which she trod
with bare feet whitened by the chalk.

By the iron machine she would sit
spinning wool
upon a loom
in the cool damp of the factory

On rainy afternoons when wheels hummed
Wendy devoured
the fleshy fruits
scattering their ripe seed as she worked.

This new, this naked loam
clean as scraped bone
delineates
a row of buttresses on which had stood

The proud iron machines
now corroded
(her quick supple hand)
and lying in their beds of earth.

The rubbish and rubble of time compress
into a strata
where is Wendy?
what is this stain in the earth?

46. The Shadow

'My skeleton and I
we are as one
and when we run
I run with my skeleton

Stride for stride
we match one another
a brother to the other
cast by the sun

A shadow with us runs
one day we will part
and say goodbye
there will be no I…'

47. Shopping

'Sir! give us extinction!
this world has never been our home
one minute we're here, the next we're gone
extinguished to decaying bone.

Fierce death always prowls
among the jostling crowds, the busy shoppers
at selection, from the giddy
catalogue of life's collection

That all dissolves to nullity
mocking fate with futility
can hospitals, temples of a material age
cure the sickness of this spiritual malaise?'

48. Dark Fossil

Baby stuck in a tar-pit is going down
he trumpets his alarms in a primeval dawn
Mother can't help him, the herd trample all around
Baby stuck in a tar-pit is going down.

Mother bellows from the edge
his eyes already know he is out of luck
his heart is an engine of pure panic
as the slow suction begins to suck.

He disappears into time's morass
his imprint revealed as a dark fossil;
in the perpetual struggle for survival
suffering is ceaseless, timeless, eternal.

49. Big Boots

'Sir! we're the lads with the Big Boots on
just wait 'till we get to the other side
there's going to be some retribution
for the injustice of your brutal regime.

You're the original tyrant! the first cause
dumb to the distress of your own creation
with you clashing suns that spawn new life
its suffering unlogged and death oblivion.

Two little girls were playing on a heath
their hearts alive with devotion and love
their innocence savagely assaulted
strangled, and thrown aside like trash.

Although our limbs will dissolve and our bones rust
yet we'll gather up our remaining strength
in defiance of our human fate
and Sir, Sir, kick-in your pearly-gates!'

50. A Moral Dilemma

So who's to blame
god, the devil or the shaman?
the way life is, it's such a shame
that predators predate, the innocent slain
it seems we have to make a choice
to be religious or profane.

So what's the truth?
the philosophers debate
the various merits of human birth
the righteous path, its moral worth
for life is pain, and Christ was kissed
by Judas, the Existentialist.

So is there justice?
who can say? what vision can see
the whole in its entirety?
for we are transient, just passing through
on a personal ticket to death's door
to be part of Creation for evermore.

51. Summer's Rose

'All the millions and millions – but she,
who is she? – the enigma of her face
is her presence here by chance or fate?
through evolution, time and space
her liquid eyes, her pastel mouth
the sexual flower of her Being.

Punctual at the laboratory, arriving
on a suburban train, her delicate hands
work with vigour, prising grit from
human skulls; the golden cascade of her hair
spilling over scrubbed bald skulls,
craniums emptied of mind and matter.

One day she will cease to be; solitary
and dark will be the universe: to find
the secret of her radiance, the essence
of her mystery, let not the blunt instrument
of life destroy her, or male psychosis slay her;
let summer roses breathe her fragrance.'

52. Dead Water Prostitute

She surfaced from the secret depths of the river
fished by men, sitting on the towpath
behind them, banks of dank vegetation
the evening suspended in a still calm.

She had become at one with nature
her skin as white as a pure lily
its pads spread to receive the sun
her faded lipstick a blush of its petals

Her nakedness unconscious as an open flower
floating on the water, deep reflections
under which hidden currents run;
dark acts of violence, fatal enigmas

The silt and mud of generation
the rank iniquities of sin;
her ancestors lie buried in country churchyards
in nearby villages; baptised by water

She, now daughter of a greater Mother
follows the course of redemptive nature
purifying with its anointment of water
the river flows through her, and flows on.

53. Pure Flowers

Seeds planted long ago
colour the present with pure flowers
where are the golden hours
of time's ripened happiness?

From time's slow organic growth
hang the swollen succulent fruit
deeds planted take root
germinate into real events.

Soft berries ripening on a stem
rich with lambent liquid glow
pressed into syrupy cordials
opiates for the hunger of the soul.

Seeds planted long ago
colour the present with pure flowers
where are the golden hours
of time's timeless happiness?

54. Dark Land

'Why take this way down a trackless lane, unwinding
through the visceral body of the world? beyond lies a land
of wretchedness and sin, the weald rain-soaked,
the level fields flooded in high summer
unseasonal weather rotting the crops, wind and rain,
rain and wind; the trees seethe with the sound of the oceans
their leaves rioting in a violent frenzy, the winds
casual strength flailing their arms; as heavy clouds hang
like congealed entrails, smothering the cardinal
power of the sun, glowering with impotent rage
its weak light extinguishing;
                      now dampness
and darkness close-in, the woods in silhouette
darken the horizon, the land become as dark as liver
as shapes indefinable merge into one;
                         in the black void
lie grain and mud, an ominous presence
the breath of decomposing vegetation;
                           pock-marked
by ragged puddles of rainwater, receding
with their reflecting mirrors, the long lane
disappears into the throat of the night
where death hovers on giant wings;
why take this way down a trackless lane
a pitted path so rough and granular
unwinding through the visceral body of the world?'

55. The Rood

'Walking the dogs around the woods
a splendorous sunset hung in the sky
like aureate fire; I stumbled to sleep
in the summer fields with deep fatigue
in the drowsy warmth of the day's heat;
when I awoke the dogs had gone
run home by paths familiar and known
and in the darkness of space and time
a colossal cross had filled the sky
higher than aeroplanes stacked in tiers
above an airport waiting to land.

It hung suspended in empty night
its face pure gold, burnished and smooth
though lit by both stars and moon
it cast no shadow, only reflected black gold
that glimmered and glowed with sinuous light
untarnished about its body and arms
as distant planes droned by its base
above the horizon, preparing to land.

I wondered what this sight could mean
from what source, what imputations?
compelled to act with righteous haste
I nailed my black deeds to a post
with a fencing hammer I had found
though still flapping, I had thought them dead
for nothing innocent has ever lived.

I stood back, perplexed, appalled
a crimson sheet flowed down the cross
I staggered back into the fields
amongst root crops and vegetables
and stared at the vision of the Rood,
for how long impossible to tell
alone in the purlieu of the night
in the silence of the fields;
what happened next I remember not.

I woke, with muscles stiff and aching back
in the chill birth of dawn
above the darkness of the land
ephemeral light shone like a jewel
and little wings baptised the air
with pure and plangent notes of song.
I stood up, and made my way back
with awkward steps, whistling for my dogs.'

56. The Quest

Stalking the quarry into the forest
fur-like, it scampers into cover
bracken-like, it changes into other

basking in the sun between tall pines
conifer needles compact and soften the floor
ants swarm alive in a lost velvet shoe.

Stalking the quarry in a glade of grass
bleached weightless bone, a tree-stump crowned
with a cushion of moss

stalking the quarry into tawny fern
wing-like, it floats over heather
a heathland of conifer candelabras.

Stalking the quarry through needled gorse
inflorescence of yellow
serried butterfly plumes

stalking the quarry through broken air
war-planes hurtle over the ling
like iron arrows.

Curled with inertia in dappled light
pine-scented, seed and cracked
pine-cones litter the floor

stalking the quarry into the forest
fur-like, it bounds into cover
pelt-like, it changes into other…..

57. Flying to the Sun

Mathematics calculated the golden section, abstract symmetry
extruded from the chaos of present time; eternal perfection
absolved from the vicissitudes of human fate; a journey airborne,
flying from the past into the future, the present in-transit,
flying through white mist, the smooth belly of the plane buoyant
through cloudscape and dreamscape, both collateral and specular
charmed by a vista of infinite cloud-horizons.

Suspended between sleep and waking
dreams are glimpsed through dense oval windows
fleeting apparitions of ideal abstractions
the human anticipation of happiness
engulfed in the nothingness of cloud-mist
until gravity takes hold and the inevitable descent begins
to the ordinariness of a plain terminal building
the same delusion of destination, the illusion of having arrived.

We never arrive; the question of existence an insoluble equation!
beneath the under-carriage the wheels are slippery
waiting for the bump of solid ground that has no ultimate reality
the invisible distils into familiar landscapes
a town, a harbour, a citadel;
ciphers manifest, built into stone
a tableau woven into the warm velure of night
a black night pulsating with the passion of cicadas…..

58. The Promenade

Down a noon-time promenade of sun and dappled shadows
beneath an arching canopy of tall dusty trees
a darling little girl in a pink dress and shock of curls
plays with her divine little black and white spotted terrier
under the indulgent eyes of father and mother;
father, barrel-chested, with a deep tan and oily curled moustache
splayed dark ink-tattoos on forearms and biceps
goads the little dog into vertical airborne leaps
to the hand claps, giggles and delight of his little one.

A white-haired matronly woman dressed all in turquoise
stops and fondly surveys the dashing scurries of the dog
the following falting footsteps of the little girl
and from the passing parade of pedestrians, as if from a carnival
a jester stands motionless, fixed, watching the scene;
his face is worn thin, without expression, like a wax-work
his hair is a wig of faded blue, around his neck a ruff;
a striped red and yellow jerkin and harlequin pantaloons
complete a comic grotesque or a sad faded clown…..

He takes from his pocket some long thin balloons, and with his life's breath
inflates the balloons, folding and twisting them
into limbs and a torso, face, ears and tail
to make a sweet multi-coloured, diaphanous sausage dog
he presents to the little one with exaggerated ceremony
eyeing the father for the reward of a coin;
the little girl in shyness runs behind her father
who accepts the gift, but no coin is forthcoming;
the jester sighs and with the long resignation of humanity continues on his way.

Father hands to his little girl this entrancing new creation
lighter than air, with the magic of a rainbow,
she, delighted, begins to play with it; but her little dog

in a fit of jealous rage and a mouthful of sharp teeth
suddenly lunges forward, there's a loud 'pop'!
clutched in her hand are just shreds of colour
gone is the mystical fond apparition
she bursts into tears; mother hugs her to her breast
'there, there, never mind! it's all part of Life's jest.'

59. Dawn Chorus

A dawn chorus of pain
seeps into wakening consciousness
as whitening daylight seeps
into the sleep of a darkened room.

Beyond the window-panes
sweet birds sing in sweet harmony
to the awakening sun; they sing
of endless possibilities

Of heart yearning fantasies
that night-dreams dissembling
know in reality
can never be.

60. Subterranean

All the lost and lonely voices
heard by no one, emptied
from the secret lockers of the soul
words of grieving and of yearning
echo through the labyrinth of time
tunnelled through the subterranean
history of human lives.

Dreams, like old advertisements
peel on dirty subway walls
as lives slide over silver rails
alive with the electric
voltage of pain
steel over steel
the speed and velocity
of underground carriages
packed with people
hurtling through labyrinthine black tunnels
driven by a chill wind
rumours and dark rumblings
building to a rapid crescendo
suddenly to emerge
into point-blank light –
the intractable reality of things
just the other side of sight
solid, impenetrable, other;
a temporary stasis;
the doors open, mind the gap –
the crowd move forward –
the everyday inhuman reality of things.

61. Moths

Lost in the darkness
entranced by light
on substanceless wings, delicate, rare

moths, ultra-violet
flutter in air
trapped in a box of luminous white

deep in the forest
framed by the night
they flit, ephemeral

in ghostly strife
like transient souls
snared in the dense tangle of life.

62. Science

'Vainglorious science! apparelled in your austere
white coats, in sterile laboratories of neon light
seeking for the quiddity of existence
you seize the particular, but fragment the whole
with a profane intellect and sharp scalpels
the matter you dissect is the spirit incarnate
of animal, vegetable and mineral.

Among a forest of apparatus, acrid chemicals
dumb mammals measured on electrodes
their animated being severed and graphed
in the vain pursuit of absolute knowledge
the illusion of a rational truth;
vainglorious science! an elemental power
squiggles beneath the tubes of your microscopes.'

63. Green Felicity

The cold sun burning like a lion's mane, trailing curdled clouds of flame
slowly stalks on cushioned pads the flat high roads to brutal death;
warrior stalking winter in a frozen fever, through raw life's temptations error
the comptometer of time clutched in his curled claws
engulfed by his own freezing shadow, spectral forms of lucid space
recess to infinity, one shape configured within another, feigning feline symmetry;
he seeks the barren woods for cover, the corrugated rise and fall of ploughed horizons,
skirting the perimeter of caravan-parks, the baroque amusement-arcade's facade
the gentle curve of the bay; casting giant shadows in a lion's frame, standing
between himself and the sun, he crouches, ready to spring.

She starts up! she is running! with silk blue skies and the shadows
of gurgling streams, the fever of sap rising in the stoic woods;
green buds open their ciphers in hedgerows, her raiments soaked in green hues
of plant hormones, plant harmonies, the oestrogen of her fabulous existence;
she is fertile, she is strong, her natural law is abundance
the fields alive and vibrant; and when she moves it is green enchantment
of sorrel, nettle, leaf and vetch; deep banks of feathered grasses,
pouring cascades of weeping willows, the lettuce shoots of hazel-wands;
she is alive! she is breath of crystal air! it is her faith and percipience
her congregation ecstatic in their worship, spreading their wings
throughout her green demesne, the green tongues of her children sing;
a liquid metronome of rain falls onto the surface of rivers,
a blessing of water, the ponds brimming their liquid eyes;
and yet she suffers intensely, throughout major and minor keys
for her brood, her children, as yet uneaten; the new born,
the unborn and the young, who raise their hands in crucifixion;
She starts up! she is running; he crouches, ready to spring.

64. Autistic

Judith hunting with the hares
with silver spears pierces
the glistening muscle of swift limbs.

Frenzied with fear, flayed of fur
bolting into fields of wheat
Judith catches the autistic ones

Crouched upon the matted earth
touching whiskers and soft fur
with hands of infinite tenderness

Breathes into their mouths, their lungs
the ripened summers of her warmth
in the wild garden of her beauty.

65. Cock-Pheasant

Cocky old pheasant! strutting your stuff
on the new mown lawn like a cat-walk supermodel
are you the big 'I' am? trying to impress
your coterie of hens, plan and dun, who feign indifference
until without ceremony you leap on their backs
in your courtship ritual; is that pheasant protocol?

You take staccato steps as you stalk your territory
furtively cocking your head, with alert beady eyes
displaying plumage in gaudy techni-colour;
you cower, spying a rival, then suddenly scoot forward
on two ridiculous spindly legs, tail-feathers hoisted
to challenge the imposter who would woo your wives!

Now fresh from a dust-bath, well-groomed and sleek
you clap your wings with a loud hoarse chortle
proclaim to the world the exhibition of yourself
nature's own pomp and vainglorious Beau –
until the guns bang and the lead-shot flies
and you and your brethren plummet from the skies.

66. Accident

Heavily pregnant, hidden in long clover
her soft pelt underbelly sliced clean open
like a caesarean, by the blades of the cutter
her young lie strewn in the grass, still alive.

Ripped from the womb of the Great Mother
their tender snouts and delicate quills
their translucent pink flesh; out of blind instinct
they begin their struggle to survive.

What accident of chance begins with birth
destiny, karma or free-will
through the swirling smokestack of time
blind fate the driver at the wheel?

67. Foetus

A foetus sleeps
on the immaculate lawn
slipped by a mare
in the early hours

Its primitive anatomy
to daylight is born
its vesselled torso
and jellied hooves.

Oblivious to life's spasm
soon to be broken
into atoms by nature
who always devours

Rhododendrons deepen
their scarlet blossom
around the sundial rotate
the sun-dazed hours.

68. A Mare's Nest

'My mother dropped
me in the world
I hugged her sides
for warmth and milk

I learned to walk
on legs like stilts
I was her pride
she was my soul.

We roamed a sea
of grass all day
I'd frisk with joy
in our pure love.

We were parted
when I was weaned
then I was broke
into a new regime

With rein and halter
my instincts schooled
my muscles trained
to carry a Lord

For many years
the burden borne
the weight carried
the work done.

As seasons passed
old injuries healed
sore were my shins
and cracked my heels.

One day a lorry
dark and green
drove me down lanes
I had never seen

Then I knew fear
it flood my heart
when we arrived
in a strange yard.

I stood quite still
should I not trust?
I'd never known
or understood…...

A gun was raised
to my head
the trigger pulled
I dropped down dead.

A tractor towed
me to a shed
my flesh and bone
to be processed.

Life is a prison
now I am free
galloping through fields
of Eternity.'

69. Sacred Wood

It is inside a sacred wood;
there stand trees from different ages
and many eternities; a young chestnut,
beneath its umbrella of silken leaves
flit delicate birds with creamy breasts
springing from nests of warm moss
hidden in the calm interior.

Strange stunted trees, old and fibrous and black
stand shoulder high amidst the green flesh of young shoots
uncurling in multitudes their parcels of starch
beneath a canopy of sturdy boughs
outstretched and strong; they stand in space and isolation
their roots spread to bite into life, to leaf.

For something is hunting in this wood
lissom with sinew, ferocious with speed;
solitary and alert by the trunks of broad trees
it tears the cloth of all mortal flesh
by brambled ditches of dark decay,
as dawn linnets chatter in the hedgerows
watching the membrane of a deep-lidded sky
turn livid vermillion, the proclamation of day.

70. Sofie

Ah Sofie, there she lies! dismembered
by the anatomy school, waiting to be collected
in seven separate wheelie-bins
filled with her offal, her bone, her soul;
long legs sprouting from one bin, her severed head wedged-in
its brain-pan open to the sky
as delicate as any fine porcelain
the hair on her face as smooth as suede
her soft eye-lashes and slack muzzle.

Suspected of a brain-tumour when first admitted
to explain the aggression of her behaviour
her swishing tail, the large intimidating bulk of her flanks
her threatening quarters and menace of her presence;
throughout the many tests of her long stay
mute to tell the vicissitudes of her life
how from a foal she was bought and sold
passed on with anxiety from stable to stable
her being insecure and galvanised with fear.

She gradually relaxed into an unexpected calm
responding to attention and daily reassurance
allowing herself to be handled carefully
until one day her door was left open, the stable empty;
she had been led away to be euthanised,
the insurance having expired; in post mortem
her dissected brain failed to reveal
any physical cause for her disaffection
her flashing teeth! her flashing eyes! ah Sofie, there she lies!

71. Spring

It was the first warm day of spring
along the field's margin no leaf had appeared
in a bare hedge lay a deer's severed head
wedged in a clump of sapling ash.

Its mask of stiff hair was drawn back
revealing roots of discoloured teeth
a bony palate dry and white
eyelids shrunk and shrivelled tight.

Inside its cranium a crusted beetle
scuttled through empty chambers of stench;
the sun was smiling, the breeze was fair
over corduroy fields young rabbits scutted

Prickled by frail seedlings of barley;
in the enclosure of a forest lay
a pool, quiescent. Its surface deep sepia,
an impenetrable fluid of leached peat

Plant mucous, pupae and larvae;
heated by the sun, pine trees sweated
their pungent resin through needles and bark;
brilliant insects with metallic abdomen

Suspended from the blur of their luminous flight
launch themselves upon transparent wings;
their skimming gyrations are transient beauty
over the pool's iris, stained ebony with time.

72. Thin Wire

These long gentle slopes
rising to the road
for generations cultivated
grassy and smooth

To the roads far side
a fenced-in pond
its surface stagnant with algae and mire
and banks of dense tangled growth.

Enclosed, teeming nature multiplies
filling space with fecundity
ready with spores to spring back –
divided only by a line of thin wire.

73. Forests

Michael in the forest, slashing with a billhook
alike the greenwood and the dead trees
his skin stretched smooth over a ponderous face
overweight, with a mouth that salivates

An inarticulate cacophony of noise
hacking at the hide of a great fallen oak
torn from the marl by a breath of the wind,
with eyes that are dead-lights, unable to grasp

The relationship between root and branch
the weight, the breadth of mortality;
he smiles into nothingness, as the wind passes
and trees crash into his mental forests.

74. Confusion

'Buzz, buzz, the talkers talk
the talking faces, talking talk
from a nebulous digital cloud
in a cacophonous Babel of Sound.

Different faces from different races
explaining, complaining, debating, relating,
smiling, frowning, glaring, staring,
behind each face a skull grimaces.

What is it you want to be?
searching for an identity
fame, or instant celebrity?
who you are is a mystery.

Male, female or gender neutral
virtual reality or real?
or a synthesis supernatural
are you the Avatar of your soul?

Buzz, buzz, the talkers talk
the talking faces, talking talk
from an anonymous digital cloud
in a cacophonous Babel of Sound.'

75. True Existence

When the dappled donkey of destiny
ambles towards the abattoir of fate
the clip-clop of his wooden hooves
resound through a world of twittering sounds.

Following sunbeams striating to the west
dropping garlands of dung for the incense-eaters
the flowers wear wrathful expressions on their faces
chanting clouds chant their insane mantras.

Munching on hay from a toxic bouquet
he brays from strong jaws indignant hee-haws
blackbirds sing duets with throaty chain-saws
though his heart in pieces shivers at the terror

He smiles a neat persuasive smile
for he carries a gaberdine umbrella;
transparent this world of perception and sense
it was never ever true existence.

76. The Wide Sea

'I cannot mend you, nor you I
eternity laps at our shores
and human love is a fleeting tide
in a sea as wide as despair;
the waves break full of breath and sound
it is not death, but life I fear.

Party mammals on the beach
calypso to a techno-beat
a transcendental trance;
waves breaking on the beach
beat the drum of their defeat
on sand of mortal oblivion.

Is there a god who made all this?
a living god of rock and stone
who will redeem our blood and bone
through rusty waters of the sea
the edge of jagged rocks that knife;
it is not death I fear, but life.'

77. Lost Mountain

'There is a mountain one should never climb
of permanent snows; there the gods reside
and the formidable view stretching to infinity
of blank white peaks one should never see --

Leaving the familiar valley behind
down there! the houses, the little church,
the villages and towns, their roads
connecting social human lives
across the valley floor; tradition,
custom, worship, work,
the familiar and the familial --

Not wind - swept, not torn jagged rocks
and perilous drops, steeps of alien ice and snow
and rocky paths of solitude
leading to higher altitudes
of freezing air and sky unreachable.

No, leave the wish for the mountain alone
where mist drifts unaware;
the mountain is unknowable
seek not the view
just close your eyes
there a different world resides
of heart and mind and soul;
the paths of human consciousness
to happiness, love and success
and look! the mountain like an apparition
has disappeared into the mist
vanished, and does not exist.'

78. Shingles

As the ordnance of the sea advances
the battery of the shore receives the blows;
far out, the general roil of the ocean
sends waves in endless repetition
the latest and the largest wave
crashes into this present moment
with spray and salt and taste of existence.

Surveying the far-off liquid horizon
the waves smaller and smaller grow
decrease with each recessive generation
from span to span; their distant ancestors
gradually diminish and dissolve
into a flat and endless solent
a sea that forgets all history.

And each wave is an incarnation
of a human face, shining through the wave
dancing on a collective tide
of home and hearth and community
each wave as bright as a flash of the sun
tossed on the wide turbulence of the sea;
the village fête, the harvest festival
the commemorative pageant, now marching to war
they vanish; recorded in sepia photographs
their faces shine through the transient waves.

79. Monuments

Slabs of white marble, scrubbed clean
decorated with the beauty of flowers
placed by fresh hands, are for the living;

The dead are dead; with no eyes
to see, no mind, no lips to whisper words
how time will erode the monuments

And tears redeposit as saline solutions
in the soil and salt oceans
as if clay could weep tears!

Time breaks the man, then breaks him down
corrupted flesh
in cathartic clean earth.

The mourners stand isolated
in the cemetery; faced by an absence
their memories a repository in the air

Distant, now fading, like clouds
that have passed before the sun
a life lighted by a brief flash of time

And eternity, that forever pours through the hour
the photographs in the photograph album
and love, that places a trembling flower.

80. The Battlefield

There is a field of eternal silence
melting beneath a golden sun
amorphous soft-snow soldiers
melt to carrion;
carrion is ripped and torn
by the beak and clawed feet of relentless Time;
rows of white crosses march to the horizon.

From the deep solstice of frozen winter
water trickles through the timeless hours
warm mists fill with a vegetable sweetness
nourishing all manner of green things
above the fields the skylarks sing
vibrating in ecstasy;
in weeping tears the melting snow
will know the tyranny of the sun.

81. Lily

Lily, Lily, named from a flower
now obliged to live in squalor
wandering through an old age
bereft of family, almost alone

Moving like a shadow in the gloom
from one dark room to the next dark room
as nervous as a sparrow in her shabby clothes
with scant possessions, just the memory

Of the sunlit childhood of a little girl
now wretched in her humanity
Lily, Lily, as sweet as the flower
of salvation, is your humility.

82. Snow Nirvana

In a paddock, a hill-side field
of sodden mud, cut and rutted by hooves
the ponies crop sour winter grasses
buffeted by sharp gusts of sleet.

A cob of big bone solemnly grazes
one eye is swollen and nearly closed
encrusted, glistening with exudates
from infection blown into the orb

By disease that rides on the winter winds
now the eye turns inward, glowing with
dull fires like marble amethyst
for its sight has flown.

Once strong and fearless, with ponderous
head, thick neck and deep chest
his aged coat flecked with iron-russet
now he is bullied at feeding times

By herd ponies, lean and brown
with two eyes to twinkle bright
and instinct of his distress
they attack from his blind side

With kicks that crack, with a swiftness
he cannot see or comprehend;
from the bins of floury meal
he wheels around in flight, his

One eye wide with alarm,
nostrils dilated with fear
of his torso's strange physiognomy
the alienation of his being.

By the gate to the field he seeks refuge,
each day waiting to be led away
to the safe interior of his own stall;
blindness was imminent; an appointment was made.

He was sent away to the hospital
the eye would be removed and the lids
stitched shut….. but the surgeon at the hospital
through compassion for the one with a coat so white

And the skill of his art, into the vacant socket
put a snow-storm dome, connecting
optic nerves with symmetry
restored his sight, and sent the cob home.

Now he stands all day on a hill-side spur
his majestic head raised, watching
the perpetual soft flakes of snow
falling over a mansion of stone

And the woods beyond
folded beneath a serene blue light;
his muzzle is creased into a smile
for all his world is tranquil and white.

83. The Sanctuary

High upon the shoulder of a hill-side, behind serried
walls of volcanic rocks, lies a little enclosed
garden of blind soil, hidden, secreted
in the shelter of a broken sanctuary.

A garden of stones and rocks
and strange extravagant arabesques
of plant growth, spinal and broody
in nocturnal moonlight, the soil dry and silvery.

Lizards slip between the moon's broken shadows
of shards, desiccated shells, bleached bones,
the garden sings in sonic tones
the wind breathes, the skin of the sea wrinkles.

Eternal time is in the breathing
it is in the breaking of numinous night
where stars crowd the vault of luminous heaven
and moon milks her mysterious light.

84. The Apocalypse

The Apocalypse can happen anytime, anywhere
even now, even here – is this it?
beyond the bay a wide expanse of sea
the smile and embrace of a perfect blue day
the waves a glittering sheen
the beach a glitter of glee
a multitude of horizontal sun-worshipers
oiled, tanning, with sun-beds and striped parasols
face the sun.

Beyond the horizon an ominous shudder
a loud boom
a low rumble and the sky crumples;
Time slips; over the waves
black annihilation comes riding-in
the future, in an instant, overtakes the present
the forms on the beach no longer human
touched by fiery points of light
the boom recedes, the sun bathes an empty bay.

For a million years the silent skeletons lay
vitrified, like fired porcelain or smooth alabaster
in rows, prostrate
as Time ebbs and flows
beneath silent starlit space
where rays of infra-red
beat down from angry dead suns;
they patiently wait
for the mystery of an Apocalypse called Love.

85. Zephyrs

The Linnet.

'When I awoke, the first thing I heard
was a linnet singing in a tree
singing notes of woe to me
'where is Madelaine, where is she?'

Her coral lips, her soul-soft eyes
as loving as the tender moon
her virtue pure as maiden snow
her voice as soft as water's-flow.

I am desolate; she is gone
into a lonely crypt of bone
her beating heart of warm desire
our love of woven fire.'

The Storm

In a clear sky of diaphanous blue
the nimbus of a small white cloud mysteriously grew
until it had filled the whole horizon
with dense vapour; light grew obscure and dim
as day preternatural turned into night
and the elements held their breath;
the clangour of an epic conflagration
began to rage; thunder rumbled
around the heavens, lightening flashed
hurling thunderbolts, splitting the air
with crashing crescendos, shaking the ground;
a wind had sprung-up from the wild sea
herding whitecaps along the crests of the waves;
on the horizon, the belly of the storm
turned bruised indigo, hiding the mountains.

One thunder-bolt struck a lonely chapel
isolated on an island, cut into the rock,
subterranean, it housed ancient relics
displayed in the crypt, tended by the villagers,
human bones, reliquaries, phials of congealed blood;
the fireball spit as it passed through
the outer-stone wall of the edifice
then levitated slowly along the central aisle
like the globe of a molten spinning sun
it struck the central column, then exploded
dematerializing, and the energy released
metamorphosied the bones, the blood
into their individual living entities;
re-animated, the spirits fled, flying
into the whirlwind of the night
where the storm still raged until first light
as gradually the skies cleared and all
became becalmed and quiet.
Listen, the birds are starting to sing
zephrys are flying on the wing
in dawn's sweet airy vapours…

Madelaine

'Who am I? a zephyr flying
released from hollow bones
from a sunken crypt of mitred stones
facsimile of what I was
a young girl, a potential bride
not a skull in an antique veil
adorned with gems and coloured beads
touched by superstitious minds
and weathered hands, a curio;
no, no; I fly! I fly!
where is the boy who courted me?
darkly handsome, he farmed bees
he wore a magnificent beard of bees

my mother, my sisters, my family
where are they? here used to be –
our old home is a ruin of stones…
but I can see! who is that little girl
sitting at the kitchen table, colouring-in
her picture book, her mother by the stove
busy with steaming cooking pots
and older sister, Dorothy, playing with her dolls
and Tolly asleep, curled-up in the corner
the sanctuary of our home, its warmth, its smells
the diamond mosaic on the linoleum
brown familiar furniture, the timeless hours
this is the time where I long to be…
father, sister, mother, it is me!
can you tell me of my tragedy
who cut the golden thread of my life?

The Bee Man

He was the Bee-Man who grazed his bees
on the carpets of wild flowers that grew
on the rocky heaths and outcrops of the island;
he had taught his bees to hum melodies
in pure harmony as they gathered nectar
from the corollas of the open flowers;
in high summer the heaths resonated
with bee-music as they worked industriously;
in the evenings, as the sun set in its meridian
he would gather his bees by walking
across the heaths and headlands
where they would flock to him, covering
his arms and legs, his head and torso,
paying homage to their king, his sweat,
the pores of his skin, in absolute
mutual trust, listening to his beating heart
as they walked back along the dusty tracks,
much marvelled at by his neighbours

a vertical walking column of bees
humming hymns to the descending sun
into the twilight, to his small-holding
a low stone cottage close to the ravine
and an orchard of hives, home to his bees.

Angelo

'I am nature, I; I do not speak words
I pick-up stones from the stoney fields
I till the soil with a hand-held hoe
I build strong walls, water the plants
on our lonely farm; we grow
good vegetables that glow with health;
deep in the veins of the earth I feel
the magma move, the pressure grow –
one day the volcano slipped out
its tongue and burnt the fields
with molten lava; it hurt the bees;
he soothed them, the Bee-Man
he sings to his bees, sings to Madelaine
they are soon to be blessed in church –
I will silence his lullabies
Madelaine is mine…
At night, when I sit in the open fields
staring at the fulgent moon
sometimes she comes too close to the earth
… her opalescence is too bright…
her shining face is too white…
Accidents can happen in a ravine perhaps…
searching for a feral swarm that has been seen
subterranean quakes have been felt
a rock falling…?
As a silent child, everyday at school
in secret I would watch her form
worship with speechless malady
Madelaine… you belong to me.'

The Running Man

When the fireball struck the lonely chapel
hissing through thick stone walls
releasing zephyrs, spirits and sprites
one person, deceased, got up and ran
without a soul, a skeleton;
once outside, he ran and he ran
ceaselessly, by day and by night
over the heaths, along stoney tracks
that criss-crossed the island
through the heat of the day
through ghostly moon-light
always caressed by a whispering sea
shorn of his fenks of flesh
his brows heavy, with eyeless sockets
his bones connected by wizened cartilage
click-clacking as he ran along the dusty tracks
causing the villagers some consternation
whenever they met him on the quiet back-roads
they pitied him and let him alone
the running man, forever running, trying
to catch-up with his lost soul
stomach-less, cannot eat his sin;
baked during the day, frozen at night
eye-sockets fixed firmly on the horizon
running away or towards oblivion
his only resolution – resurrection.

Vendetta

After the deed was done, dead in the ravine,
when the Bee-Man did not come to collect his bees
in anxious anticipation they hummed
hovering above the wild herbs and flowers
until the sky darkened with the setting sun

and they dropped to the earth, one by one.
At daybreak, ending their lonely vigil
their fur still damp from the night-dews
the bees took to the air; they have found
their fallen king, and swarm in a dense cloud
of mournful melancholy above his form.
He is buried now in the crypt of the lonely chapel,
soon to be joined by Madelaine, a suicide,
and a village in deep mourning. It is fate,
uncommon death, in life where death is common.
But one bee had witnessed all, collecting
nectar near the ravine; in a language
known only to bees, communicated
with the common throng; after
the funeral obsequies, they gathered
in a cloud above the open heath; villagers
heard the low resonation of their hum
as they discoursed in bee conversation
the plan and execution of their revenge.
As Angelo was sitting cleaning his rifle
in his front garden, before an open door,
the farmhouse at the end of a long straight track
looking up, Angelo thought he saw, unbelieving
a dark silhouette advancing down the track,
the Bee-Man, miraculously resurrected from the dead!
his bees had assembled in the form of their king,
head, arms, torso and legs, buzzing angrily.
Angelo shrieked, as the apparition advanced
gathering speed, flying over the ground
in panic he fired his gun, but the shots
passed harmlessly through the bees, who
immediately dispersed into a fuzzy cloud
as Angelo ran towards the open door
they overtook him and engulfed him
and with a hundred sharp stings pierced his skin
with venom; as he lay dying from apoplectic shock
he tried to mouth a silent prayer, to Madelaine

but his lips were too numb… then
his body underwent a strange metamorphosis;
his feet and hands twisted into knobbly roots
his head became a haemorrhage of stiff green hair
he started to grow into the earth
sprouting shoots… screaming hysterically.
Now he stands, a gigantic towering
thistle of artichokes, a curio
whose excessive growth is believed by locals
to be caused by the volcanic soil
and its deep, deep roots
heated by the magma below…
His throat is routinely cut when the heads of the
artichokes are removed; prized by gourmets,
they are boiled in stainless steel saucepans
in the kitchens of the island's best hotels
and served with butter sauce.

Night Linnet

'When I awoke, the first thing I heard
was a linnet singing in a tree
singing notes of woe to me
'where is Madelaine, where is she?'

Her soul a mirror of the moon
shining silver in solitude
extinguished by my jealousy
black womb of night without that 'she'.

I am dislocate, lost to time
trapped in an alien world sublime
yearning magma of desire
congealed in veins of liquid fire.'

Resurrection

'I am conscious of a new sun rising
as dawn's first light reveals
a golden path across the breaking waves
to a distant island washed by the sea;
caressed by zephyrs and the sun
a fusillade of nightingales opened their throats
singing of Madelaine with lyrical refrain;
her spirit had metamorphosied
into a verdant bush of vibrant flowers
delicately scented, consummated
by the tender industry of the bees
as they hum their hymns in harmony
on an island, or illusion, on the sea.'

86. Onement

'I walked into the garden of my dreams
the beauty of the flowers shone like truth;
the mistress of my soul was near, burning
bright and unpossessed, she had dark eyes
and darker hair, as beautiful
as the deep-cupped rose
exhales the fragrance of her soul
into a tangle of nocturnal growth
dense with dream and dream-desire
when beauty like a comet flares
in dream-time when time is lost
when loving eyes in silence stare
though truth and beauty are both false,
my love for you is pure and true.

As light subtracts from primal night, self
splits from self; dawn defines a garden wall;
then sparrow-like our dreams flit through
the tangled briars into passing day
the self divided from itself, dissembling form
in substance splits the eye with light
the beauty and the beauty seen
by eyes, that cannot themselves perceive
then self from self cannot be true
but variegated, an outward show
where beauty its own truth deceives
with infinite divisibility;
though self itself can never know
my love for you is pure and true.

The sky is fresh with morning dew
releasing scent from the salt earth;
the mistress of my soul is here
burning bright and unpossessed
she has fair eyes and fairer hair
the beauty of a perfect rose
though the earth is desert and the garden closed
truth and beauty are all gone; the furniture
of the forests smashed to splints
and clouds have burst into liquid tears;
through pain of self grow the flowers
of God; as a snake takes a fledgling
from its nest, and time devours our consciousness,
my love for you is pure and true.'

87. Illusions

The fires of Autumn are all aflame
red, yellow and orange, the leaves
seared by time, unloosen
from the crowded canopies in the woods.

Illusions bared to the husk of bark
her beauty that transcended form
deep, shining, pure
darkened by cruel fires

Her liquid eyes, blackened and burnt
by the savage flames, her frail
elusive frame, her silvery dreams
are as powdered ash.

The elm, the beech, the sycamore
the antlered crown of the aged oak
lie rotting in long shanks on the floor
weathered and cracked and felled.

As wistful as the scent of woodsmoke
her fragile spirit sleeps, bereaved
the bitter ash of consumed fires
regenerates the buried seed

Into deep tickets of Evergreen
the laurel's pure and virgin leaves,
birdsong ringing in the woods
in the mists of a silver dawn.

88. Golden Leaves

An expiring sun
glancing through the trees
sets on fire
all the golden leaves

Of the russet woods
in their autumn dress
in the dying time
of the year's distress

In the dying time
of the planet's sun
when the universe
on its course has run

When the falling stars
from their cosmic home
fall back unto
the original womb.

89. Hunters

The hunters hunt
the eaters eat
behind a pretty girl's smile a skull grins.

Food is power
let the dog see the rabbit
into the world's grinding jaws

From the stain of death
burgeoning forests
metamorphosis

Innervate into brilliant birds
wild grasses of the meadow
from insensible matter

Of oscillating stars
colour, light, dynamic vessels
their rainbow sails.

A ball thrown against a brick wall
a group of playing children
who burst into laughter.

90. The Labourer

In extreme old age, crawling like a crab
on two bent legs and two straight sticks
with hands cramped by a life of toil
slowly lifting vegetables in the garden

His clothes soiled, his possessions negligible
but the root-sap that wells in his eyes
that sparkles and shines, has seen
the green seasons one another succeed

In their eternal cycle, and knows
a lifetime's communion with the soil
that was his provenance, and will be his inheritance,
where his heart will burst with its timeless seed.

91. The Fall

'I plucked a leaf, to help nature with her Fall
the dried leaves crunching beneath my feet
the green leaf already withering in my hand
a fate that will encompass all.

The green leaves of life are brief
one by one they relinquish the tree
that were nourished by her felicity
She, who is the Mother of us all.

A separation that in time will come
Time, the immortal golden One
a time that will encompass all;
I plucked a leaf, to help nature with my Fall.'

92. Wasp

Protesting against an invisible membrane
cold, vertical, frustrating your will
to rejoin summer and the summer's sun

your yellow jacket striped like a tiger
thorax and abdomen vibrating with ire
feelers skate over polished window-surface

all of summer's ripeness beyond the glass
blue skies, orchards and basking warmth
glucose of apples, plums and pears

suspended from the trees, fermenting in the grass
an intoxication of paradise
your tiny frame filled with pulsating desire

frantic for summer, you will be as One
when your jacket is empty and the summer has gone
(the earth your body, your flesh pieces of the sun.)

93. The Ash Tree

'A songthrush sings
in a tall ash tree
the ash tree stands
in our old house

The walls are invisible
the roof is lost
the foundation stones
are covered in moss.

So all things change;
our love is gone
the door through which
our children ran

They are changed
into earth again
an ash tree and
a melody of song.'

94. Cloud Sonnet

When clouds collide, like giants that walk in front of the sun
naked, insubstantial, Atlas mountains of vapour
spun from existence by quick-silver Time
they drift into oceans of cerebral blue
with ragged edges that catch on nothing
not knowing whence or where they came from
drift-on, over cities, wheatfields, harbours,
river-valleys and suburban gardens
always seeking the far horizon; billow high
into aerial space, vistas of smooth molten marble
where jets criss-cross thin vapour trails
suddenly dissolve, then reappear again like ghosts;
when clouds collide, like giants that walk in front of the sun
expire, fall to earth with a blessing of rain.

95. The Hare

As the air thickens, and light grows dim
crude thunder crashes through the heavens
lighting pirouettes like a demented dancer
rain slashes the reeds and river.

An old brown hare leaps for cover
along the banks of water-fowl and swan
haunted by the primal terror
shelters beneath a hawthorn's crowning blossom.

The sky brightens as the storm-clouds clear
a watery sun illuminates the fens
the old brown hare on the open fields
settles into her form, and disappears.

96. Cherries

'Where the cherry leaves
shade orchard paths
and the sun plays warmly
through the trees

And my eye is filled
with the yellow sky
and black flies haunt
the songthrush dead

Then let my blood
so cherry red
stain the red rose
of eternity

And I will remember
the summer's leaves
gently swaying
at the tips of the trees.'

97. Being

'We went down to catch the horses
through the swing of an iron gate
down into the valley, into the freezing winds
soughing over the low wolds, bare woods
and thorn hedgerows, wan fields
and shuddering skies, pastures matted
with dry long grasses blanched by winter,
the wind funnelled between field-slopes
twigs and branches littering the lanes
snapped from dark towering trees,
everything exposed to a searing raw cold.
   They were standing in a huddle.
by the gateway, fetlock deep in mud
set against the wind's constant flow
siphoning precious breath from our lungs
with frozen hands we slipped leather halters
over large whiskery heads
there was a wildness in their eyes
their manes grown long and tangled
with rough winter coats, they swung
their hindquarters as the gusts shifted
and jinxed all the way up the hard road
the wind chasing their heels,
by the high stone wall we led them
until we reached the shelter of the yard
where they subdued into a sudden calm;
we unloosed them into their barn
out of the wind, and as the night froze
in unlit darkness they stood like statues
smelling of warmth and straw and dung.

We waited for the rain, holding the horses
in full harness, in the draughty shelter of the stables
beneath the door-way of a stone arch;
brilliant cloud billowed above tree-top
and high house-gable, trailing heavy showers;
time stilled, listening to the drum of rain pelting,
light became cold and bluer, and then the sudden whoosh
of a shower passing, the horses impatient and nervous;
it ceased imperceptibly, the drip of rain-drops
lessened and stopped, the grit on the gravel path
sparkled with sunlight, as sparrows chattered and bathed
in the puddles, squabbling over straw wisps,
boisterously nesting under the eaves.
   We rode out through the iron gates
down narrow country lanes, clouds over our shoulder
overtaken by their sweeping shadows
undulating across fields and sheep pasture
we rode through stone villages, awakened
by the clangour of iron-shod hooves
past dry stone walls, farm-yards, spring gardens
bright viridescences opened by sunlight, a stand
of beech trees high on a hill cast
deep shadows, lynchets cut into its green side;
trotting up inclines, we glimpsed the horizon
wolds engulfed by sweeping showers
riding into wide open skies, the wind
pure and clean, we hacked in single file
along the elevation of a long straight road
leading up to a level common; there we broke
into walk, the horses steaming in their breath
and their sides; walking across the common
feeling the new spring turf beneath them
as one ride, they suddenly broke into canter
racing the clouds across the skies
there was a wildness in their eyes…..

The cockerel crowed, and day began
over the wide open window of morning
the clean milky smell of the country-side
everything sleeping in a white mist
cloaked with the soaked dews of dawn;
sap was rising with the oestrogen of spring
the country-side greening with lush fertility
all sprouts and shoots fresh and young
now the mist dazzled in the sun's presence
the wolds lifting their white veils.....
fenced in a paddock of post and rail
out of the mist trotted a colourless horse
a flea-bitten grey, its form emerging
from the pallor, he stopped abruptly,
with flared nostrils and a loud anxious snort
then suddenly turned, and galloped into the mist
his stomach tight with colic, his gut
already twisted, the drumming of his hooves
resounded around the field, invisible,
pummelling the ground, he kicked
against death tightening in his entrails
until late morning when his body was found
dead, prostrate, staring at the sky
there was a wildness in his eyes......

After the day's strong heat, as the evening distilled
the call was received; the horses had escaped
into the cornfields; we drove down a hard jolting track
through gateways overgrown with thick hedgerows;
they were standing chest high in the young corn
parted like a sea of green virility, they had
trampled its stalks into skeins and whirls
leaving broken paths of their misdemeanour
in their wake, imprinted in the grain;
we drove them back as a herd of guilt
crashing through the corn, their eyes wild,
snorting with their own and each other's fear

back along the track to the fenced enclosure
and rough pasture of their broken paddock;
the far distant worlds had hushed into twilight
leagues of fields, stone-walls and hedgerows
woods and farms and silent villages
the sky flushed with a strong menstrual light
igniting the heavens with pure crimson;
time annihilated time; in the nexus
creation shared one single living breath
before the wolds dimmed as the world rolled....

The chug and cough of an invisible tractor
slowly turning-over earth into furrows
as white smoke from distant stubble-fields
melt into the whiteness of infinite space;
inside, the house sleeps the domestic sleep of winter
dogs curled around the warmth of a cooker;
a clock ticking on the mantle-shelf;
outside, the drizzle presses onto rooftops,
distant villages, farm-yards scoured by cattle
the wolds invisible and the world lost;
near walls of wet ivy, by a house of stone
a starling's sweet descanting whistle
softly dies into silence and stillness;
out of mist and obfuscate darkness
loom window-panes of golden light
this is our house, this is our home.'

98. Harvest

Nature is a living spirit, a bronze wind
a pool of autumn trees;
horses steam from out of the forests

Trotting along old bridal paths
their flanks flexing with muscular tension
legs reaching with forward impulsion

Sinew and tendon and syncopation
driving through the skin of the weald;
guided by a sympathetic rein

Metallic shoes of civilisation
flash upwards from the yielding earth;
old blackened hearths, distant fires

Fields fading in a harvest twilight
a parish gathered to evening worship
the sweet warm breath of humanity.

99. A Fresco Fiasco

He gazes at the Madonna with more than heavenly devotion
Padre Dominic, a novice, suppliant on his knees, with eyes raised
to the lovely eyes and face portrayed in the Fresco; it is mortal love,
well marked by his new congregation, especially one Leonardo Luccio
'big noses smell big roses', a local trickster and ugly bug
whose bragging and fanfaronade frequent the bars and cafés
with his ragazza, a Miss Pampolini, actress and cabaret 'artiste',
bearing more than a passing resemblance to the Portrait,
they devise a plan to liberate the Father from his church silver
kept under lock and key in his private chambers.
Sabrina, her twin brother, once a man, now a woman
with more than a passing resemblance to 'his' sister
a former drag 'artiste', wearing chiffon, a tight skirt and blonde wig
totters down cobbled streets to attend evening Mass;
secretly in love with the handsome Father
she worships with a sincere devotion, wears high-heels
just to please her vanity! lonely Deity, you need humanity!

Father sees her beneath the Fresco after Mass one evening
as if she had just stepped from the shadows of the painting
dressed almost identically in a simple cloak, Miss Pampolini
confesses her desire to take holy orders, if he would teach her;
is this a miracle? entranced, he leads her to his chambers
for further explication; she says she adores heavenly priests;
but first he must check the vestibule for penitent sinners
who wish to confess; finding none, returning to his rooms
good gracious! Miss Pam Pampolini is in a bikini! she has dis-robed
ready for her seduction! is that a 'sign of life' or a divine revelation?
she pleads her devotion, can she kiss the silver chalice?
Father Dominic, embarrassed, promises to pray for her soul
then ushers her promptly from the premises, much to her chagrin;
later, at the Cabaret, when she relates to one Leonardo Luccio
how simple chastity had thwarted his villainy
he viciously licks his ice-cream, utters pronouncements
of prolix profanity! lonely Deity, you need humanity!

In the market square, youths kick around a football,
ride in circles on their scooters; Geena looks after her father's stall
every evening attending Mass, secretly in love with the handsome Father;
after a day of pouring rain had washed-out the markets
water seeps through the stone walls and mortar of the old church,
through the porous gesso of the Fresco, to emerge as a tear
from the eye of the lovely Madonna; a miracle! seen by Geena
as she enters the church, she reports to Father Dominic in bashful tones
what she has witnessed; he is entranced by her simple faith,
her clear eyes and sincere face; he has found his Madonna!
(of the fruit and vegetables); he vows a silent prayer
they will be together until the resurrection, and then
for all eternity, as time tells the story, Amen!

At Mass that evening, in his congregation, he spies Sabrina
fresh from the beauty parlour; assuming her to be 'her' twin sister
marks with approval her sincere devotion (extraordinary to take
off one's clothes in order to worship ancient relics?), gratified
she is seeking salvation; later, walking the rounds of his parish,
musing on the mystery of love and the mystery of the cobble-stones
the nature of miracles invisible in the shadows
he chances upon a commotion in the street of the Cabaret;
it is a woman doing a rumba beneath the bougainvillea
as a band of brass musicians play a blaring salsa
there's a strange familiarity about her demeanour
with more than a passing resemblance to the Madonna
(except for the short-skirt, high-heels and blouse)
it is Miss Pampolini celebrating the summer evening
always a free spirit, applauded by a gathering crowd
she responds with increasingly suggestive gyrations
as they clap in unison to this 'sign of life', Sabrina
suddenly appearing in the doorway, apparelled in drag,
saunters-up to 'her' sister on the beat, they proceed
to dance a tango along the street, two twinned 'Madonnas'
cheek to cheek, each with demonstrative feet, the crowd
are ecstatic! Father Dominic watching this living Fresco,
with a brimming heart, bestows a silent blessing

upon this company, then crosses himself to preserve
his sanity! lonely Deity, you need humanity!

100. The Journey

'All move down, make more room on the bus
standing room only, jostling cheek by jowl
a various assortment of people get-on
punch their tickets, hold-on to a rail;
a mother with her daughter from a shopping trip
a fashionable teenager checking her look
an Asian housewife texting on her phone
a dark haired woman nursing her baby
an African scholar mouthing from a book;
the bus stops as more people get-on
at the back, a young woman with prosthetic legs and feet
talks to a group of garrulous old men
in a cassock, a sober priest dressed all in black
looks on; the next stop, people waiting in a queue
commuters eager to make their way home
tired manual workmen wearing worn denim
a gaggle of giggling girls from school
a business-man in a regulation grey suit
a white-haired grandmother with a face of resignation;
another stop, more people squeeze-on, impossible!
the doors just managing to dovetail-shut
as the bus moves off into the dusk
on its scheduled run to the last zone
everyone included, no one excluded
one human family on the same journey
with a destination, on their way home.'

101. Workshops

The saw cuts, a large disc
of carborundum steel, whirled to a blur
its edge slowly biting a groove
into a rough block of quarried stone.

With effort of toil the fly-wheel revolves
the bench slides forward into the blade
the tension exact, and the timbre
of the note expelled a strident whine

Reverberates through the outside yard
into the cold. A fine mist of spray
distils a rainbow, cooling
the action of metal through stone

As work passes through the hours
blocks of ashlar, measured by fatigue
to be built into a human future
wait on pallets, precise and smooth.

Beneath a roof of galvanised tin
and the din of busy workshops
arc-lights cast a fragile warmth
into a winter's late afternoon.

The last cut is made, the waste is removed;
as workmen depart in the dark to their homes
a solitary cube of pristine stone
sits resplendent on its bed of wet iron.

102. The Lanes

A big fat pigeon flops onto the fence
flung by the wind's casual strength
luminous clouds brighten to the sense
an aeroplane growls in the distant heavens.

A hawk straddles a pigeon on the lawn
with a hooked beak eviscerates its soul;
leaves like a snake spiral and coil
chased by sharp gusts of wind down the lanes.

Sheets on the washing-line sail and billow
as cars slipstream over the horizon
above shines the blue light of heaven
it's time already for the school run.

103. Yellow Hammers

A family of yellow-hammers
dazzling on wing
flit across harvest
fields of stubble.

In nests of silken
woven grass, the scribe
leaves hieroglyphs
on ivory shells.

Embossed with flints
strange and misshapen
the crushed shells
on the timeless ocean

Gleam with a
chalk-white radiance;
a dog's eye is filled
with live movements

A hare receding
on a ploughed horizon
the land ribbed
like a rib-cage

And the sky is an arch
through which
innumerable suns
shed their days.

104. Chrysanthemums

He lived in a fertile valley of woods and sweet pastures
his house secluded, by a healthful flowing river
but nature had been false, corrupted his body
with crippled genes. He walks his garden paths
with a crumpled bent back, face and hands
as rough as bark, collecting windfalls from a single tree.

He wears a white hat in the warm haze of late summer,
pushes a barrow of small ripe apples
given freely to friends and to neighbours
with no accusation in his bearing
in handling the smoothness and coolness of apples
against the crudescent hide of his skin.

He tends the borders of dahlias and chrysanthemums
examines the large globes of their petal-studded heads
rests, and wonders at the marvellous power
the deep mystery of their perfect beauty
giving and receiving, like the sunlight
receives and is blessed, by the sunflower.

105. Breathing

After the furnace of noon has stunned
the green wheatfields, and the sky's fierce cerulean
cooled into evening, trees and hedgerows
festooned with their greenery, relax and breathe;
in the deepening shadows a majestic chestnut
stands like a cathedral, illuminates
the twilight with its ghostly candles,
all doors and windows flung wide open;
above the rooftops, around a village square
the perpendicular silhouette of a church towers
amidst massed foliage of cloudy trees
their spreading canopies arboreal breathing
in the penumbra of a warm summer's night;
from the square comes the chatter and clatter
of restaurants, bars bright with talk and laughter
vivid with their social company;
the surrounding narrow streets lit with neon
reveal the warm glow of honeyed stone
as cars drone by out on the border
searching the dusk with their raking beams
beneath a fine gauze of stars
and a heaven of deep lucidity
the trees breathe, the leaves breathe,
the green-fields breathe, the night air breathes.

106. Sand Castles

One print of tracks upon the sand
one track across a sandy heath
of needled scrub and sun-tanned grass
dry heather-bells and flowering gorse.

Amidst the tussocks of an uncouth tract
a seething anthill's swarming mass
labours over tinder littering the ground
on the barren hills feathered with pine

A thousand castles dissolve on the beach
as families parade along the promenade
past pastel chalets and ice-cream vans
empty shells upon friable sand.

The salty mollusc and soft seaweed
imprinted trace of trackless time
the swell and roll of the surge beneath
the purple heather on a diamond heath.

107. The Voyage

She sails, slipped from her moorings by a tug
of the wind, leaving behind the solid quay
her smooth sleek hull slips through salt-water
into the tide of a mystical sea.

In the intense radiance of early dawn
where distant mountains hang like veils
somewhere a volcano smokes and smoulders
earth's molten belly beneath buoyant waves.

Passing stumps of broken lava
like giant dragon's teeth littering the strand
gliding over silken sheen of water
to what fabled islands? what distant lands?

Waves bob the bow; a breath of the wind
sings a chanson through the sheets and the sail
like the siren call from a beautiful girl
who waits on a shore at the end of the world.

108. Dreams

'Drifting through still water-meadows
reeds trembling with the river's tide
hidden by islands, at the wood's edge
a bank of dense damask flowers

Breathe scent into the warmth and balm;
lapped by the rise and flow of water
through the drift and sifting of ooze
light flashes over petrified fishes

Shimmering with the beauty of pearl
their mouths agape, half sunk in the sand
in resonance with ancient harmonies
they rib the wave-patterns of the strand

Their rose fins and pink fleshes
embalmed in the mists of a golden sun;
for ever may travellers through these isles
be held by the kindness in their eyes.'

109. Gnats

'Gnats are like tiny
heavenly bodies, sparkling
over sheets of sliding water
they do not collide,

But strain against
the evening breeze
interchanging, interweaving
ever moving, ever blind.

Only I see their ceaseless motion
with my One eye, reflecting
black night watches eternally,
white stars that ever glide.'

110. Parliament of Birds

A confederate flock of tiny birds
burst into a holly tree
with wing and feather, zips and trills
from perch to perch they delicately spring.

Whistling speech and banting chatter
through the dark viridian leaves
in a parliament of sound
around a barbarous holly tree.

From disparate families, of good colour
through snow-glare and frozen light
they flit and swoop, in fluid confluence
foraging for berries like pure blood-drops

By an ancient garden wall
the earth hammer-hard, ponds sheeted glass
their tiny ruby hearts patter
for they have traversed the dazzling Void.

111. The Consecration

Allowed to play in the graveyard, a garden and a public park
of an elegant Gothic church, while parents and adults
of the wedding party, the bride and groom and their many guests
wearing the sheen of silk, dressed in pressed suits
pose for formal photographs; the children, a riotous assembly
chase each other around tombs and gravestones
treading on their unseen guests, on a glorious May morning.

The paper-confetti already strewn on the pavement, they find
beneath an ornamental cherry-tree confetti of pink-blossom
the tree being in full bloom; they stretch and jump, trying
to pluck the laden boughs, just out of reach;
seeing their mischievous intention a casual stroller
resting on a park bench, approaches the tree
and seizing the trunk proceeds to vigorously shake it.

With a shudder the tree sheds all of its flowers
in a mass of pink petals that cascade down
over the heads and glee of the children
who unselfconsciously dance and whoop;
boys and girls receiving nature's own blessing
a consecration that life through time engages,
a celebration of their future marriages.

112. Dancing with the Dinosaur

Rotund like a Buddha or Earth Mother
sitting on her hams, the loving 'mamma'
watches with delight as her little girl
dances entranced with her dinosaur
in rhythm to the beat of an amplified band.

A weightless Tyrannosaurus Rex
of inflated fluorescent aluminium foil
with glad eyes and a big goofy grin
he jigs up and down, as 'mammas' finger's flex
twitched on the end of a piece of string.

Her little girl gambols on the spot
shifting her weight from foot to foot
(still wearing her harness 'tiny-tot')
with the face of an angel, pony-tail and fringe
she dances with her dinosaur king.

Eye to eye, hypnotised
by the side of the stage, on the park's green
as the girl-band play their electric guitars
theirs throats singing sweet Siren Songs
full of the promise of burgeoning summer

To cascading chords and the beat of a drummer
beneath bright sunshine and brilliant skies
the spirit and the senses synchronised
the little girl dances for pure joy
with her dinosaur toy, in the Festival of Summer.

113. The Dancer

As she steps into the arena
long eye-lashes beating
open and shut

a piercing blue sky
her eyes transcendental
her scent a dangerous perfume

fashionable and elegant
she moves with ease
placing each foot

with poise and precision
onto thin leather soles
of soft yielding shoes

waist, bridge and heels
a perfect fit
for her svelte deportment

a cushion-cut topaz
of piercing blue
their only ornament

set in a nest
of baby-blue down
step by step

onto the ball of each foot
she moves across the plaza
of people and fountains

incised polished marble
her instep steps over
step by step

with rhythm and rhyme
moving like a dancer
through space and time -

114. Eyes

The wood's shadow guarded
the hidden corn, the bark of a dog
from a distant village, in the stillness
before the storm.

The cloud's shadow compassed
flocks of wheeling starlings
around the stone steeples
indestructible energy.

The hill's shadow startled
the consciousness of eyes
burning in the hedgerows
their buds alert and alive.

The moon's shadow harboured
boats floating by the wharves
the texture of walls
chalk-clouds dissolving.

The pool's shadow mirrored
the eye's of a thrush, open
as beads of dew brightened
the morning stars staring.

The violet shadow pointed
walkways flooded with bone-light
the growth of magnetic plants
the giant abstract of the sky.

115. The Trance

Sunstruck by light
a rippling sheen
circles pool shallows

as the mill-race glides
the demoisells dance
across the water's skin

sound beyond hearing
the perpetual flow
of water in motion

cascading over
the curtain of a weir
the friction and plunge

of a river pouring
its crystal oration –
the weir in a trance.

116. The Close

The close lay sequestered
in cool shadow, long and narrow
flanked by a noble cathedral
of smooth veined marble
and the rough crumbling walls
of an ancient town house
decaying in its magnificence.

No doors or windows exit
from the close, no one comes
and no one goes, only
the chirp and chirrup of the sparrows
echo in this space
of tranquil enchantment.

Their brown tawny backs slip in and out
of an ornamental boxwood hedge
clipped, low and serpentine
in shape, a testimony
to nature's living presence
framed by close high vertical walls
a narrow aperture of bright sunlight
opens onto a distant street
busy with the hustle and bustle
the footfall of many passing feet
pursuing life's pressing vanities.

What season, what hour, what time passing
of ancient seismic calamities
carved into stone, the blue-veined marble,
the magnificent edifices
the mighty engine of the earth
arrested at the sea's edge
with quiescent ossified lava-flows;
since the first light of dawn

the hidden presence of a close
silence and cool shadows
the chirp and chirrup of the sparrows…

117. Jay-Bird

A jay-bird in a white wood
of solitude, on frosted air
flew through a glade of purest light
through darkness purer than deepest night.

His plumage feathered with bright jewels
circling, with open wing
between the ceiling and the floor
calculus of cosmic law

The downy indigo of space
soft suns rolling on soft moss
the locomotion of the spheres
the spangled volume of their mass.

Transparent zebras galloping
casting shadows sidereal
diatoms spiralling in a swirl
diamond-ticking spokes of light.

The circuit of a white star
amplified in a coiled shell
kinetic ladybirds that whirl
turbine of acoustic tides

The drama of a grand design
a gleam of absolute radiance
hares scampering in a frozen dawn
a nebula of twinkling ice

A clarion of matchless blue
the shadow's name upon the flood
the crystal chrysalis of snow
touched by the burning light of God.

118. Time

Time unloosens the knot, lets go;
rooks wheel above dense thickets
of bare woody growth, congested with their raft
of nests and timber and twigs, with cracked voices
in the tall trees talk of Spring
with soft questionings, they know.

Time unloosens the soul, lets go;
dead empty husks lay all around, withered
dry stalks levelled to the ground
in One direction, as the winds decree
succulent flesh of fresh green leaves
flow through the woods like an underground sea.

Time unloosens the knot, lets go;
a fallen wild cherry, couchant, twisted
with splayed giant boughs rooted
into earth, like tidal foam
into the sky above
bursts into flower with white snow (God's love).

119. Nightingale

'I sing for love
to the moon, to the stars
liquid arias

invisible, unseen,
from a lonely canopy
a bible of trills

ascending in scales
as the night shines above
its true colours of love

an angel of glory
singing to Be
I set you free'

120. The Golden Hind

The sea is blue
the sea is green
the sea is grey

The presence of a pensive
golden hind, silently stepping
into early light.

The dawn is red
the dawn is grey
the dawn is white

The presence of a pensive
golden hind, silently stepping
into golden light.